Star SCENE

Totally Jonas!

Up Close with Today's Hottest Band

D0117115

JOE

KEVIN

NICK

By Michael-Anne Johns

Scholastic Inc.

New York   Toronto   London   Auckland   Sydney

Mexico City   New Delhi   Hong Kong   Buenos Aires

PHOTO CREDITS

ISBN-10: 0-545-11083-1
ISBN-13: 978-0-545-11083-9

Published by Scholastic Inc.
SCHOLASTIC and associated logos are trademarks and/or registered trademarks of Scholastic Inc.
Copyright © 2008 Scholastic Inc.
12 11 10 9 8 7 6 5 4 3 2   8 9 10 11 12 /0

Designed by Angela Jun
Printed in the U.S.A.
First printing, September 2008

CONTENTS

INTRODUCTION

KEVIN JONAS!
JOSEPH JONAS!
NICHOLAS JONAS!

You can almost hear the roar of cheers from the Jonas Brothers fans when you just say their names. Not since Hanson, and before them the Jackson Five, have brothers made music lovers jump to their feet, sing along, and dance, dance, dance.

Though the Jonas Brothers were off to a slow start in 2005 and 2006 when they first appeared on the scene and released their debut CD, *It's About Time*, things definitely changed in 2007. They changed record labels, yes, but that wasn't all. The Jonas Brothers' die-hard fans stuck with Kevin, Joe, and Nick. Even when the guys didn't have a single out on the charts, their Jonas-ites were demanding information about them — from fan blogs and chat rooms, fan sites, and, most important, the teen fan magazines. Kevin, Joe, and Nick were constant cover guys in the magazines. Interviews with the Jonas siblings were worth their weight in gold!

Well, that means the following pages might help solve the national debt — you'll find all the interviews, quotes, facts, fun, and pinups you ever could want. So read on and get ready for a Jonas-good time!

THE ROAD TO SUCCESS

Up until 2005, the small township of Wyckoff in northeastern New Jersey was best known as a friendly community where every one of the 16,000 population was known as a "neighbor." Wyckoff's known as the "Garden Town" of the Garden State, and the beautiful tree-lined community lives up to it. Little did the residents know there was a hurricane coming — not of the weather kind, but of the musical kind!

THE JONAS BROTHERS BUZZ

Hurricane Jonas — Joe, Kevin, and Nick Jonas — appeared on the musical Doppler reports in the year 2005. But music was part of the Jonas family's life way before that! The brothers' parents, Kevin, Sr. and Denise Jonas, belonged to a singing group that often traveled the East Coast to perform at small venues. So, back in Wyckoff, the soundtrack of the Jonas household was constantly playing. For as long as they can remember, Kevin, Joe, and Nick were singing, playing musical instruments, even writing lyrics, but it was Nick who first made the professional move.

Legend says that Nick was singing in a barbershop in Wyckoff and was discovered by a music manager. Soon the six-year-old Nick was commuting from Wyckoff to New York City — he was appearing on Broadway in such mega hits as *Beauty and the Beast, A Christmas Carol, Les Misérables, Annie Get Your Gun*, and *The Sound of Music*. Then, when Nick was nine years old, he and his dad worked together on a song, "Joy to the World (A Christmas Prayer)," which was included on the 2002 annual Broadway *Equity Fights AIDS* album, *Broadway's Greatest Gifts: Carols for a Cure Vol. 4*. Kevin, Sr. sang on the CD, but Nick had made a demo of the song, and it came to the attention of Steve Greenberg, who was then the president of Columbia Records. It just so happens that Greenberg also was the man who discovered the powerhouse sibling group Hanson, so his "ear" was tuned to chart-toppers.

JONAS BROTHERS HIT THE BIG TIME

Initially, Greenberg was interested in signing Nick as a solo act, but then he found out that Nick's older brothers, Kevin, and Joe, had co-written songs on the demo CD. When the boys paid a visit to Columbia's Madison Avenue offices in NYC, they sang "Please Be Mine." Greenberg signed the boys, as a group, immediately!

Kevin, Joe, and Nick headed into the studio to work on their debut CD, *It's About Time*. The transformation was amazing. Initially, Nick had been a Broadway singer, and the first songs written for the demo CD had been Christian rock. Now the guys were creating a punk-pop CD. With a huge fanbase already tuning into the guys via MySpace, it looked like *It's About Time* would be an instant hit.

The first single, "Mandy" did make MTV-*TRL* history. The song was about a girl that Joseph used to date. Though they were no longer seeing each other romantically, she remained friends with the entire Jonas family. Actually, Joseph recalls, "She was Nick's best friend when they were little. But she got older and I guess I saw something in her differently and we started dating. And it was really cool, but it didn't work out. We're still like the best of friends."

"Mandy" was the Jonas Brothers' first video and they filmed it as a three-part story, each of which was released consecutively on TRL. Shortly after that, Jonas Brothers songs began appearing on TV shows and soundtracks — "Time For Me to Fly" on the *Aquamarine* soundtrack, "Mandy" featured on *Zoey 101: Spring Break-Up*, the theme song of *American Dragon: Jake Long*, and many more.

JONAS TIME

On June 25, 2007, the Jonas Brothers headed out on a three-month U.S. tour. They performed at large theaters, small clubs, fairgrounds, and the like. It was like a family road trip because the boys' parents and their little six-year-old brother, Frankie, joined them on the tour buses.

The tour was leading up to some major Jonas Brothers events. On August 7, their CD, *The Jonas Brothers*, was released. To celebrate the day, Nick says, "Our dad rented a yacht the night our album came out. We sailed to the Statue of Liberty. It was a blast."

On August 17, they appeared on the "Me and Mr. Jonas and Mr. Jonas and Mr. Jonas" episode of *Hannah Montana*.

In the following months, they performed on TV shows, won awards, and on October 18, they headed out on a 54-date concert tour with Miley Cyrus on the Hannah Montana: Best Of Both Worlds tour. Next came their own headline jaunt, the Look Me in the Eyes tour, which started January 31, 2008. Then they kicked the summer off on July 4th with their Burning Up tour. In the meantime, they were busy in front of the cameras, too. In May 2008 their Disney Channel reality TV series, *Jonas Brothers: Living the Dream*, premiered, and in June their first TV movie, *Camp Rock* aired on the Disney Channel too. That's not all. They also committed to a TV series on the Disney Channel. It's called *J.O.N.A.S!* and it's about three brothers who are special agents for the government—Junior Operatives Networking as Spies. They are undercover as a hit rock band, but when they aren't performing, they are super spies!

Now the Jonas Brothers are part of the Disney family, and using the super success of their CD and TV projects as a springboard, they put "taking breaks" behind them. It's work, work, work, but they love every minute of it. "It's exciting!" Kevin told a reporter.

With all this happening, it really looks as if it's JB time . . . and it's about time!

MUSICAL NOTES

THE JONAS MELODY OF LIFE

Singing is my life . . . *I think I have always known that. It's just something that since I can remember, I knew. That is something that everybody always says, but for me it is true. From the age of two, I was telling my grandma I had to practice because I was going to be on Broadway. — Nick*

The first song I remember singing . . . *was probably a song from Peter Pan. I used to watch that every day, I know "Neverland," that song, " I know a place where dreams are born . . ." That is the song I sang. — Nick*

I think I always wanted to make people laugh . . . *That is my job — to be a comedian all day. I loved the show All That, and when I was younger I always watched it. I was like, "One day I am going to be on that stage and make people laugh." Then when I was singing around the house my dad was like, "Joe you have a great voice and you should sing." I was like, "You know, OK." I love what we are doing right now. People love it and it is really cool. — Joe*

Jonas Brothers is . . . *the album of our dreams. We're getting to make the music from scratch — from the drums to the bass to the guitar to the vocals. We're picking songs that we want to be on the record and we're all playing and singing, so we're really excited because this is the album that we really wanted to make. It's also exciting because this is the first record we made that I really, really enjoy listening to on my iPod.* — *Kevin*

Jonas Brothers is . . . *just the Jonas Brothers being the Jonas Brothers, which we think is really cool. We create the music that we want to create and people enjoy it, so it's awesome.* — *Nick*

Jonas Brothers is . . . *just us, updated.* — *Joe*

We get our song inspirations . . . *from a lot of different places. A lot are from personal experiences.* — *Nick*

Little brother, Frankie . . . *says he kind of wants to make his own band. He hasn't warmed up to the idea of being in our band.* — *Joe*

My musical inspiration is . . . *my dad. He was so good. We were always playing [music] around the house. — Kevin*

We grew up listening to . . . *old-school music. Some of our favorite musicians are the Beatles and Switchfoot. — Joe*

I've always described our sound . . . *as music on Red Bull! — Kevin*

Writing together . . . *feels like the most natural thing we could be doing. When we write a song, we get in a triangle. I start playing the chords that we've chosen over and over, and then we'll keep going around in a circle until we have figured out the lyrics for the song. — Kevin*

Nick is . . . *the powerhouse vocal. He's just got this young, soulful voice that catches everyone's ear. — Joe*

Joe just has . . . *this really cool, smooth rock voice. He really knows how to get the crowd going. — Nick*

Kevin is . . . *the one that holds us all together. Joseph and I are the singers and take turns on keyboards and percussion, but Kevin mostly plays the guitar and that's the part of the group that we need — he's the glue that keeps us together. — Nick*

Our fans . . . *are awesome! They're more like our friends. We start recognizing people, too, especially on our MySpace.* — *Joe*

Music is . . . *like my life. I guess music to me is very special. You have to have music [to express your] feelings — every time that you are happy, you can, like, put it into a song. There are songs when you are happy, and there are songs when you are sad. It is just everyday things like that.* — *Joe*

Music is . . . *like life in general. When you walk outside, you know, you hear things and especially when you are in the studio a lot of times, you start hearing beats with everything you do. Everything becomes a song, and that is really how our life has become.* — *Kevin*

THE SOUNDS OF THE JONAS BROTHERS

DISCOGRAPHY

Albums

- *It's About Time*
  (Columbia Records) August 8, 2006

- *Jonas Brothers*
  (Hollywood Records) August 7, 2007

- *Jonas Brothers: Bonus Jonas Edition*
  (Hollywood Records) October 30, 2007

Singles

- "Mandy" — *Zoey 101: Music Mix* and *It's About Time*
- "Year 3000" — *It's About Time* and *Jonas Brothers*
- "Poor Unfortunate Souls" — *Disney's Little Mermaid Special Edition* soundtrack
- "Kids of the Future" — *Meet The Robinsons* soundtrack and *Jonas Brothers*
- "Hold On" — *Jonas Brothers*
- "S.O.S." — *Jonas Brothers*

SPOTLIGHT ON KEVIN

Kevin Jonas is known as Mr. Charm; he has the charisma and smooth appeal that attracts millions of fans. Besides being a guitar hero, Kevin is the grounding force of the sibling trio. Nick has called him "the glue" that keeps the group together. Nick and Joe often look to Kevin to keep things level and reasonable in a world where life could be pretty chaotic.

Kevin knows how to treat people, especially girls. He's always a gentleman. For example, he recently told a teen magazine reporter, "I think guys should still open a door for a girl every chance they get, every time. They should try to take care of a girl as much as possible. She's like a princess, no matter what."

Well, believe it or not, there's another side to Kevin. While a lot of people think he's King of Hearts, Kevin is the first to admit that he isn't always perfect.

"I've always been scared of failing," he confesses. "I hate to disappoint those I care about — I want to make them happy. I'm such a people-pleaser, especially in relationships. I'm definitely working on it. I try not to be a pushover, and I'm really making an effort to voice my opinion more."

When it comes to girls, well, Kev doesn't have the "I can date anyone" attitude. "I'm afraid of getting rejected by girls," he admits. "And rejection can be the worst in music. I have to remind myself that although it may be risky, I'm doing what I love. I also know that if you don't take chances, then you'll never know what will happen!"

KEVIN TIDBITS

- Kevin has a collection of guitars and other musical instruments, including four acoustic guitars, six electric guitars, one bass guitar, and two drum sets.
- One of Kevin's acoustic guitars was handmade. The wood is from Africa and is very rare.
- Kevin admits he thinks *High School Musical*'s Ashley Tisdale is awesome!
- Kevin is a neat freak — "I hate not having clean clothes. If I have a shirt and I wore it, it needs to be cleaned. I'm really weird about it."
- Kevin's fave tech toy is his iPhone!

SPOTLIGHT ON JOE

According to his mom, Denise: "Joe is just quiet, very sweet, but he has a mischievous side. When he was little, he had an adorable face, big brown eyes and puffy hair. . . . Joseph was very attached to his Barney, and I was like, we have to get rid of this thing. I had my friend bring it to the trash and Joseph saw her. He said, 'Why do you have my Barney?'"

Well, that was then, this is now . . . Joe's Barney is long gone, and he's dealing with the "shy" side of his personality.

"It used to bother me that I was shy," he says. "I was always the one playing it safe, never coming out of my shell because I was afraid. I've since grown up — I'm outgoing, and I just like to have fun!"

But some things never change. Joe may have been traumatized by the puffy hair thing, because he admits, "I tend to worry about how I look! It's good that I have my brothers around to reassure me. If they weren't there, I probably wouldn't get out of the bed in the morning! I'm also always checking the mirror because I'm afraid that I have something in my teeth. It's an insecurity!"

JUMPIN' JOE

- Napoleon Dynamite is the kind of movie that makes Joe laugh.
- Joe's mom recalls one early romantic gesture — "He bought this girl he likes a pretty little stone that said something on it and put it in a heart box and gave it to her. She rejected him!"
- Joe's nickname is Danger.
- Joe loves girls with accents!
- If Joe were president, he would make sure "I'd have a fresh pair of socks every day!"

SPOTLIGHT ON NICK

Though the Jonas Brothers are the hottest band around today, life isn't always picture-perfect. Sure they have to deal with adult problems that other teens don't, but one day Nick came up against a challenge that could have been life-or-death.

In the fall of 2005, the guys were on tour, preparing the way for the release of their first CD, *It's About Time*. It was a long, stressful tour, but Nick, who is usually the Energizer Bunny, began feeling tired, listless, and moody.

"I started experiencing weight loss, a bad attitude — things that weren't me," he recalls. "So after the tour we went to the doctor and found out I had diabetes. The first thing I asked the doctor was if I was going to die. It was crazy."

Not so crazy — Type 1 Diabetes is a major concern with kids in the U.S. today, and if undetected, it could cause all sorts of medical and physical problems. When diagnosed, the disease requires constant vigilance — daily insulin injections, careful diet, exercise, and regular visits to the doctor.

Nick had to spend three days in the hospital to get himself on the right track, and during that time he learned about the disease — and how to live with it. "It was hard," he says. "There were times I just didn't want to have it. It was a learning process."

One lucky medical advance Nick has taken advantage of is something called the OmniPod. It is a pump that is attached to his skin that constantly drips insulin into his body, so he doesn't need to give himself shots.

Because Nick realized so many kids across the country are also living with Type 1 Diabetes, he and his family decided he was going to go public about his illness. So at a concert at the Diabetes Research Institute's Carnival for a Cure, Nick made the announcement, and ever since then, he has worked hard to get the message out — deal with the disease and learn to live your life to the fullest!

NICK'S QUICKIES

- Nick loves to listen to Johnny Cash.
- Nick loves the word "Excellent!"
- Nick thinks Corbin Bleu's Chad was the coolest character in *High School Musical.*
- Nick hates it when someone pretends to be him on MySpace.
- Nick loves that designers give the group clothes — "Free clothes! I haven't actually purchased any clothes in about a year. We're blessed!"

"OUR FANS ARE AMAZING. THEY'LL DRIVE ACROSS THE COUNTRY, STAND OUTSIDE UNTIL WHO KNOWS WHEN. WE APPRECIATE EVERYTHING THE FANS DO." — *Kevin*

"WE ARE HAVING A GREAT TIME DOING THIS. WE LIKE TO SEE PEOPLE ENJOYING OUR MUSIC AND HAVING FUN AT OUR CONCERTS" – *Joe*

"WE TAKE TIME TO MEET EVERY SINGLE ONE OF OUR FANS IF WE CAN. WE LOVE OUR FANS AND WOULD BE NOWHERE WITHOUT THEM." — *Nick*

"WHEN WE'RE SITTING AT HOME, WE DON'T WANT TO BE THERE. WE WANT TO BE OUT PLAYING OR WRITING SONGS. THIS IS WHAT WE WANT TO DO." — *Kevin*

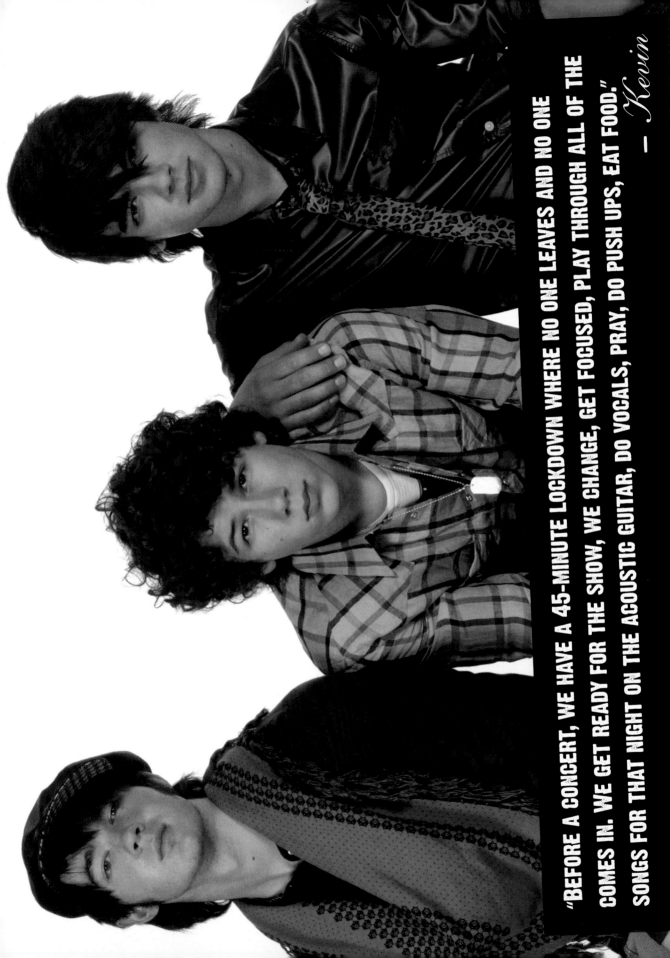

"BEFORE A CONCERT, WE HAVE A 45-MINUTE LOCKDOWN WHERE NO ONE LEAVES AND NO ONE COMES IN. WE GET READY FOR THE SHOW, WE CHANGE, GET FOCUSED, PLAY THROUGH ALL OF THE SONGS FOR THAT NIGHT ON THE ACOUSTIC GUITAR, DO VOCALS, PRAY, DO PUSH UPS, EAT FOOD."

— *Kevin*

"THERE'S NO JEALOUSY—I THINK WE'RE GOOD ABOUT THAT; WE'VE BEEN DOING THIS FOR A WHILE NOW AND IT'S NOT AN ISSUE. OUR PARENTS ARE AMAZING; PEOPLE AROUND US ARE AMAZING. [WE ALSO KEEP] EACH OTHER IN CHECK—THAT'S REALLY IMPORTANT." — *Nick*

THE ULTIMATE JONAS Q&A

ARE YOUR FRIENDS SURPRISED BY WHAT IS HAPPENING TO YOU GUYS?

Joe: Yeah, it is pretty crazy. It is weird sometimes, but we love it when we walk into our local Starbucks in our town. We can easily go hang out, and then we get stopped about three or four times by, like, nobody that we know.

Kevin: People who we used to go to school with come up and say, "Hey, you guys have a ringtone." We are like "Yeah, we do," and that is really strange.

Joe: They are looking through their phone and are like, "Wait . . . The Jonas Brothers . . . 'Mandy'. I went to school with them!"

NOW THAT YOU ARE WITH HOLLYWOOD RECORDS, YOU HAVE MOVED OUT TO LOS ANGELES — DO YOU LIKE IT?

Nick: Yeah. We rented a house to stay in while we're recording the new album, and it's so much fun.

WHAT DO YOU LIKE BEST ABOUT LOS ANGELES?

Kevin: The weather — it's 75 degrees even in February. That's nice. You can go swimming all year round. The people are really cool. It's a lot of fun.

WHAT DO YOU MISS MOST ABOUT NEW JERSEY?

Nick: We'll be back there all the time, so hopefully we won't miss it too much while we're out here. We'll be [back] there soon enough.

Joe: One thing they don't have out here [in L.A.] is Rita's Italian Ices. We used to have one right next to our house and it was so good.

WHAT'S THE SILLIEST STORY YOU'VE SEEN WRITTEN ABOUT YOU?

Kevin: There was one that said I was married. I was like, "No, no, that didn't happen."

Nick: There was one that said that I was shy, which I'm not, I just don't talk as much as my brothers.

WHAT'S THE SILLIEST QUESTION YOU'VE EVER BEEN ASKED BY AN INTERVIEWER?

Joe: "What do you think about scoliosis?" We kind of answered like, "Well, I know it's not good. You should probably get it checked out."

DO YOU PREFER ANY ONE TYPE OF VENUE — CLUB, STADIUM, ARENA — OVER ANOTHER?

Nick: I definitely like to mix it up. We can play a huge arena, and then we can go to a small, 100-person show in a little theater. It's cool to mix it up. Of course, big is nice, but it's all fun.

DO YOU GUYS STILL USE THE INTERNET FOR GRASSROOTS SUPPORT AS YOU DID IN YOUR EARLY CAREER?

Joe: Totally. Every single day, we're on MySpace talking to fans. They sometimes use crazy online lingo that we can't understand, but my dad's the best when he reads them to us. He'll say, "Yo, you guys are hot." So we do it every day, and we like to keep doing it ourselves. We like to go online and write to the fans ourselves, and go on the chat boards and talk to fans and get to know them. It's just awesome.

WHAT'S THE FUNNIEST FAN EXPERIENCE YOU'VE EVER HAD?

Kevin: There's been so many. I don't know.

Joe: When we were in Nashville, we came from a long day of interviews. It was midnight. And we stayed in this motel because every other hotel was booked since there was a big award show that night. So we pulled up and we were so excited to go to bed, but all of a sudden this car screeches up to us. The window rolls down, and this older lady looks at us and says, "We wanted to find you." I just looked at my dad and was like, "What's going on?" And they asked if they could take a picture and we said sure. And then they said, "Don't worry, we won't come to your rooms. But we know you're staying in 816 and 817. We've been sitting here for two hours." So we went inside and we told the manager to change our rooms. It was so funny. I thought we were going to die that day! Another one is when we went to one school and I don't know why, but the girls would cry. I was like, "Why would they cry?"

Kevin: Just to meet us. They were banging on the door screaming . . .

Joe: . . . like for an hour-and-a-half and one girl was crying. Skipping school just to meet us.

Kevin: She got suspended. We actually have this one fan from North Carolina. We have been doing shows [all over], and she has actually been flying to our shows.

Joe: She has actually been driving sometimes.

Kevin: She drove twelve hours [one] day . . .

Joe: . . . just to see us, so we actually brought her onstage and sang her a song. She loved it. She thought it was the greatest thing.

Kevin: It made her day.

DO YOU HAVE ANY SPECIFIC FEARS OR PHOBIAS?

Joe: I'm afraid that when I'm asleep that somebody might want to break into my house and punch me. It's called the Afraidthatpeoplearegoingtopunchyouphobia.

Kevin: It's more about feeling like you disappoint people — that's the fear I have.

Nick: We've gotten this question a lot, but I don't know if I'm afraid of anything. Maybe of not succeeding — but that's more of a doubt than a fear.

HAVE ANY OF YOU READ A BOOK IN THIS PAST YEAR THAT YOU WOULD LIKE TO RECOMMEND?

Nick: I've started on the whole *Chronicles of Narnia* series. It's really, really good. . . . But I have always loved the *Magic Tree House* books. They are my favorite. I still read them. That lets you know how much I love them. I started reading them when I was in third grade.

Kevin: I definitely agree with Nick. *The Chronicles of Narnia* books are great books. I've been reading them after not having read them since middle school . . . it opens your eyes to a whole other aspect of it.

Joe: I would have to say *A Wrinkle in Time*.

PART OF THE JONAS BROTHERS LEGEND IS THAT KEVIN LEARNED HOW TO PLAY THE GUITAR BY READING A BOOK CALLED *TEACH YOURSELF HOW TO PLAY GUITAR*. THE STORY WAS IN YOUR ORIGINAL BIO — IS IT TRUE?

Kevin: Yes! I actually faked sick that next day so I could stay home and continue learning. They left that part out of the bio. Yeah, I mean Nick actually plays drums. We both play guitar and piano, so we do that in our set when we do it live and stuff which is really cool. I have plenty of instruments. My parents are very musical. They are always teaching me new things. We have a piano in the house and guitars. We have tons of guitars, and so it is very cool that we get to just write songs.

DO YOU HAVE ALL–TIME FAVORITE SONGS?

Kevin: It may have to be "3x5" by John Mayer. There is a line that says "There is no 3x5 this time because I want to see the world though both my eyes," and I had to think about it. [I wondered] "What does he mean by that?" And then I realized that if you have to take a picture then you have to close one of your eyes to actually take a picture, and he just wanted to take it all in. I was like, "Whoa that is awesome." It was one of those songs that made me think and really inspired me and the way that I write songs.

Joe: Switchfoot, they have a song. I think "Only Hope" is what it is called. I love Switchfoot, and I love that song. It is really cool.

Nick: My all-time favorite song would have to be "Superstition" by Stevie Wonder. I love that song. It is so good. I bought a new cell phone the other week, and the first thing I did was bought the ringtone for "Superstition."

YOU ARE ON THE ROAD A GOOD PART OF THE YEAR — IS THAT HARD ON YOU GUYS?

Kevin: Wow, I love it. It is so great. I get to travel the world and do music. It is so cool. This year I got to see a lot of the U.S. I think my three top favorite places are L.A., Boston, and New York.

Joe: Yeah, same for me from what I have seen so far. Yeah, they are beautiful places.

Kevin: I really enjoyed Boston. It was a great town. Every time we have been able to go we have actually been able to go and hang out downtown for a while.

Joe: I was like, "I did not know that Harvard was in Boston." When I saw it I was like, "Whoa, it is huge."

WHEN YOU FIRST STARTED AND WENT ON TOUR, YOU TRAVELED BY CAR — WHO DROVE?

Kevin: We are all backseat drivers. . . . Joseph and Nicholas are the worst backseat drivers. They are like, "Slow down, slow down!" And I will be like, "I am going the speed limit, leave me alone." They are so bad.

ARE YOU GUYS GOOD AT READING MAPS? DO YOU GET LOST?

Joe: Oh, yeah, we get lost!

Kevin: We have to count every day how many U-turns we take. It is bad.

Joe: There was one time when we were coming home from a show and we were going to go out to eat and we are [looking for] a nice restaurant. You know, when you go on tour you have to make [the best of] what you got to eat because you [usually end up going to] McDonald's. So we drove I think two hours away from our hotel by accident. It was pretty funny. It was pretty bad. We were on the road and we all fell asleep and we wake up and we were still in the same place. They said we had to turn around and we drove like halfway there and halfway back.

YOU GUYS HAVE BEEN QUOTED THAT A GUY NAMED "JOEY BAG OF DONUTS" IS ONE OF YOUR BEST FRIENDS — WHO IS THAT?

Joe: That is his nickname.

Kevin: It was so great because he actually flew out for the shoot of our first video. He is this Hollister, Abercrombie kind of kid. He is big with blond hair and blue eyes, and he just looks like a total surf dude.

Joe: He flew out, and he ended up being one of the main character bullies in the "Mandy" video.

Q: HOW DO YOU GUYS SETTLE YOUR DIFFERENCES?

Kevin: Sometimes there is the awkward moment when you are just like, "Oh, whatever."

Joe: We're brothers, and we are always going to have some quarrels. Nick always gets upset if I wear his socks. He always gets upset and freaks out and he is like, "Joey, you were in my dresser."

Kevin: I mean, we usually just get along. We get along pretty well because we are also a band. We know we can't just get upset [with] each other and hold grudges while you are on stage. It is not going to work. We know how to work it out. We know things are petty and we are just like, "You know forget it."

Q: IF YOU WEREN'T INTO MUSIC WHAT DO YOU THINK YOU WOULD LIKE TO PURSUE?

Nick: Sports. I am a sports fanatic. I love sports. I think I am probably one of the biggest Yankees fans alive.

Q: HOW MANY YANKEE GAMES HAVE YOU SEEN?

Nick: Oh, this is the best part. Check this out, I don't go to very many games, but I watch every single game on TV, every single one. So I am pretty crazy about the Yankees. When I can't actually watch it live, I TiVo it. . . . I am also a die hard Dallas Cowboys fan. I don't tell many people that because I will get made fun of.

WHAT ARE YOU MOST LOOKING FORWARD TO OVER THE NEXT YEAR?

Nick: I am really looking forward to how this whole thing is going to unfold. I truly believe that this [CD] is going to be a success and a great record that people will really enjoy. I just can't wait — people have been waiting for it to come out for so long. I am excited to see my dreams come true. I am excited to do what I love.

KEVIN'S FACT SHEET

FACTS

FULL NAME: Paul Kevin Jonas II

NICKNAME: (Who gave it to you & why) don't have one

BIRTHDATE: 11/5/87

BIRTHPLACE: Teaneck, New Jersey

CURRENT RESIDENCE: Hollywood, CA

RIGHTY OR LEFTY? Righty

HEIGHT: 5'11"

WEIGHT: 135 lb

HAIR & EYE COLOR: brown & hazel

PARENTS: Kevin and Denise

CHILDHOOD PETS: Cocco (dog)

BEST FRIENDS: John Taylor

DESCRIBE YOURSELF AS A CHILD: Super hyper

DATING

GIRLFRIEND/BOYFRIEND: Girlfriend

MOST ROMANTIC DATE: Gentlemen don't kiss and tell

TURN ON: love a girl with good style

FIRST DATE: was great

WORST DATE? haven't had one yet

WHAT MAKES YOU ASK FOR/WANT TO GO ON A SECOND DATE? if I had a really good time

DO YOU LIKE A GIRL TO ASK YOU OUT?(FOR BOYS): No!

WHAT WOULD YOU BUY A GIRLFRIEND/BOYFRIEND FOR HER/HIS BIRTHDAY? Jewelry

EVER DATE A FAN? If I get to know her/yes but always looking.

FIRST

KISS: don't kiss and tell

THEME PARK VISIT: Disneyland

MOVIE: Jungle Book

CONCERT: MxPx

CD/ALBUM BOUGHT: MxPx

MAJOR PURCHASE Jeep

CAR: Toyota Camry

GIRLFRIEND/BOYFRIEND: can't remember

JOE'S FACT SHEET

FACTS

FULL NAME: Joseph Adam Jonas

NICKNAME: (Who gave it to you & why) Danger—because I'm crazy

BIRTHDATE: 8/15/89

BIRTHPLACE: Arizona

CURRENT RESIDENCE: California

RIGHTY OR LEFTY? Righty

HEIGHT: 5'8"

WEIGHT: 140 lb

HAIR & EYE COLOR: black & brown

PARENTS: Denise and Kevin Jonas

CHILDHOOD PETS: Cocco (dog)

BEST FRIENDS: Amelia

DESCRIBE YOURSELF AS A CHILD: amazing, funny, adorable

FIRST

KISS: was great!

THEME PARK VISIT: Six Flags Over Texas

MOVIE: Homeward Bound

CONCERT: Kenny G.

CD/ALBUM BOUGHT: Britney Spears

MAJOR PURCHASE: Nike Dunks

CAR: can't drive yet

SCHOOL STUFF

BEST/FAVE SUBJECT—WHY? math-because I like to challenge myself

FAVE TEACHER—WHY? John Taylor—he's helpful

DO YOU FIND MATH EASY/HARD? hard

ANY MATH TIPS? don't forget your calculator

SCIENCE DISASTER: I once broke 2 beakers on the floor

DID YOU LIKE HISTORY? no. . . I love it

WHAT HISTORICAL ERA WOULD YOU LIKE TO VISIT? WHY? the 80's-good music, great food

MOST EMBARRASSING MOMENTS IN SCHOOL: getting called to the principal's office the first day of the new year

NICK'S FACT SHEET

FACTS

FULL NAME: Nicholas Jerry Jonas

BIRTHDATE: 9/16/92

BIRTHPLACE: Dallas, Texas

CURRENT RESIDENCE: California

RIGHTY OR LEFTY? Righty

HEIGHT: 5' 6"

WEIGHT: 105 lb

HAIR & EYE COLOR: brown hair and brown eyes

PARENTS: Kevin and Denise Jonas

CHILDHOOD PETS: Cocco. He's a dog

BEST FRIENDS: Maya, Kibble, Mandy, Vandanye

DESCRIBE YOURSELF AS A CHILD: very creative and independent. I loved to sing.

FAVES

SPORTS: baseball

TV SHOWS: Lost, Sportscenter

MOVIES: Finding Neverland and Better off Dead

ACTOR/ACTRESS: Jake Long

BAND/SINGER/MUSICIAN: Stevie Wonder

FOOD: I love steak

DRINK: 7-11 Slurpee

CANDY: gummy worms

SANDWICH: Italian hero

HOLIDAY—WHY? Thanksgiving because of all the good food

FAMILY TRADITION: Putting up the Christmas tree

MISC.

FAVE AFTER SCHOOL SNACK: Twinkies

COLLECTIONS: I collect baseball cards and I have been for the last 3 years

EVER BEEN IN A FIGHT? No, sometimes I'll get mad at people but fighting is pointless

ADVICE ON HOW TO AVOID THEM? Don't let your temper control your action

DID YOU EVER SAVE YOUR MONEY OR SPEND IT: I would save up for a while then I would spend it.

CRUSHIN' WITH KEV, JOE, & NICK

Love, love, love . . . the Jonas Brothers are definitely all about love! They sing love songs; they love their fans, family, and friends, and, needless to say, they are the most-loved boy band today! Read on for more Jonas details on matters of the heart.

HALLOWEEN HEARTACHE . . . WELL, STOMACHACHE

Once, Joe had a date on Halloween and he recalls, "I bought this huge costume to make my crush laugh. I was dressed up as a cowboy riding a bull! I liked it because it has this button, when you pressed it, the cowboy suit blew up and became really huge. [My date] was dressed up as a milkshake. It was really awesome! We went trick-or-treating all day. But we ate too much candy, and we both wound up getting sick!"

LOOKIN' FOR LOVE

"I don't have a girlfriend right now, but I'm always looking," confesses Nick. "I want a girl who understands my crazy schedule, who will be there to support me, and who can make me smile."

THE SOUND OF LOVE

"For some reason, a girl's voice [attracts me]," admits Joe. "Interesting voices. . . . I like accents, too. Definitely!"

DREAM GIRL

"Someone that's totally, completely cool," Kevin describes his Ms. Right. "Like, they can just talk to you like we're regular people. I really like it when they're not impressed. Or they put on the face of not being impressed!"

BUTTERFLIES?

"When I want to ask someone out, I get really excited," says Joe. "Of course, I get a little nervous beforehand, too, you know? But I get more excited than anything else around the girl because I just really want to ask her."

FIRST MOVE

Kevin knows how to get things going. "I'm a talker, so I talk to people. I'm not afraid to walk up to you and just start talking to you. I won't try to make you laugh, because it's not going to happen — I'm not funny at all."

NICK'S DREAM DATE:

"I would buy box tickets to a Yankees game and watch the Yankees beat the Red Sox."

JOE'S DREAM DATE

"It's all about the surprise. I like to have fun, so we'd go bowling."

KEV'S DREAM DATE

"I believe the best date would be going to New York City and having dinner. A restaurant we like is La Mela. Tables are set up in the street covered with overhanging lights. Then head to a Broadway show. End the date by walking her to the door."

GIRLS ARE FROM VENUS – BOYS ARE FROM MARS

Nick wants girls to know that there is a big difference between them and how guys look at things. If he could tell girls one thing, it would be, "Guys can't read minds!"

AN OLD–FASHIONED BOY

"I really love dresses," admits Nick. "I like a girl who looks like a lady."

THE LOOK

"I'm a sucker for blonds and redheads," spills Kevin. "But sometimes, it's also the smile that gets me."

THAT CERTAIN SOMETHING

"If [a girl] is talented, that's really cool," Joe says. "Every girl has something special about her. And it's cool if she can share it with everyone! . . . I like girls who like to have fun, too!"

JO-BROS ON THE ROAD

For the past two years Nick, Kevin, and Joe admit that much of what they've been doing is reading road maps! They've hardly had a chance to unpack the moving boxes from their move to their new home in L.A. Actually the boys have been on a constant musical whirlwind across of the country.

The **Miley Cyrus/Hannah Montana: Best of Both Worlds** tour began on October 18, 2007, and ended on January 8, 2008. In the few weeks the guys had off, they had a little time to relax and remember. Of that fandemonium, Joe says, "[It] never gets old. It's crazy when police have to hold back girls, but awesome."

It became pretty obvious that the guys could pack an arena, so they signed a two-year worldwide tour deal as headliners. That stint started with the **Look Me in the Eyes** tour, which ran from January 31, 2008 through March 29, 2008.

ON THE ROAD . . . AGAIN!

No sooner had the guys unpacked from the "Eyes" tour and the premieres of their Dis[...] Channel's TV movie *Camp Rock* and reality series, *Jonas Brothers: Living the Life*, they picke[...] up their gear and headed back out on the road for their 38-city **Burning Up** tour from Jul[...] 2008 to August 31, 2008.

Whew! Oh yeah—they also celebrated the release of their third CD while they were o[...] the road in August 12, 2008. "It's going to be a fun record," Kevin said before it hit the sto[...] "Everyone keeps asking us, 'What's the attitude? What should we be looking for?' I'd say i[...] a hopeful, good-time kind of record. It brings a smile to our faces." And Nick added, "I thir[...] we've gotten a little better as musicians, so maybe the chords of the songs are a little different, more mature. But it's still fun, pop/rock music and lyrics."

Where to next? Any place in the world, because the Jonas Brothers are the most famou[...] sibling music group since Hanson. It's all good for the guys, and Kevin sums it up with, "We[...] wake up every morning excited because we get to do what we love."

FUN ROAD NOTES

- The guys have become Wii Guitar Hero masters since they challenge each other during backstage downtime.

- If you take a peek in the cabinets on the Jonas Brothers tour bus, you'll find Chewy SweeTarts (Nick's fave), mini-chocolate bars (Joe's fave), and Butterfingers (Kev's fave).

- The bunk beds on the bus have been nicknamed "condos" by the brothers.

- When Jo-Bros played their home state of New Jersey on the **Look Me in the Eyes** tour, the 12,000-seat venue sold out in 2 minutes!

- The Jo-Bros recorded their new CD while on the road with the **Look Me in the Eyes** tour. They turned their tour bus into a high-tech recording studio.

JONAS BROTHERS . . . CAMERA TIME!

Movies, DVDs, TV series, TV specials . . . Jonas Brothers' super fans can't get enough of on-camera time for the guys! And it looks as if the House of Mouse Ears (Disney) seems to agree. It's hard to believe that Kevin, Joe, and Nick actually had the time to do anything while they were in the studio working on their new CD and touring around the world. But they did!

JONAS BROTHERS—LIVING THE DREAM

Spring 2008, Disney Channel

The reality series was filmed during the boys' Look Me in the Eyes tour, and it caught their onstage and offstage antics. It's the first time fans got a peek at the entire Jonas family—especially the Bonus Jonas, little brother Frankie.

"We've been filming a really cool reality show," Kevin told a TV reporter. "They've been following us pretty much the entire tour on and off, so it'll be fun for the kids to see what we go through day in and day out and how absolutely crazy it is for us. It's really exciting."

Frankie, the Bonus Jonas
"He's really making a name for himself," laughs Kevin. "When we do events now, he can't really go anywhere because our fans know him so much they start screaming his name."

CAMP ROCK

June 2008, Disney Channel

In Toronto and a remote part of Canada, Kevin, Joe, and Nick spent seven weeks filming their first TV movie, *Camp Rock*. Unlike their reality series, *Living the Dream*, the guys do not play themselves. They are a band called Connect Three, and Joe plays the lead singer, Shane. Kevin and Nick play bandmates Jason and Nate. After a music video onset meltdown, Shane is sent to a rock 'n' roll camp to sort things out.

"Shane is not happy he's going there," says Kevin. "We canceled our summer tour, and he's got to find himself again. We know this will be good for him no matter how much he hates it."

What the guys didn't hate was that their costars were some very talented, very pretty girls! Meaghan Jette Martin, Demi Lovato, Anna Maria Perez de Tagle, Jasmine Richards, and Alyson Stoner hold up the female side of the movie. The plot centers on Demi's character, Mitchie, who desperately wants to go to this prestigious music camp. According to Joe, newcomer Demi "has an amazing voice, and she's a great actress and has become a good friend of ours. We're writing with her for a record she'll probably release at the end of the year."

When asked about his character, Nate, Nick explains, "He's a lot like me in the sense that he knows what he wants and knows he has to keep his head on straight. . . . He's kind of the exact opposite of Kevin's character, Jason. The dynamic there is really cool."

J.O.N.A.S!
September 2008, Disney Channel

Once again, Joe, Kevin, and Nick combine a little bit of fact and a little bit of fiction in the TV series *J.O.N.A.S!* They play an up-and-coming rock band touring the country in a rickety old bus. But while they are performing and winning fans wherever they go, they have a big secret. They work with their secret agent dad to fight evildoers! The name J.O.N.A.S is their band name, but it also stands for Junior Operatives Networking As Spies! Not even their mom knows their secret identities, but there are a few who have suspicions.

As of this writing, *J.O.N.A.S!* is scheduled to premiere in September 2008.